THE BLUEPRINT OF PRO-ACTIVENESS AND PRODUCTIVITY

CRAFTING HABITS FOR SUCCESS

DR. MINAKSHI BANSAL

Made with ❤ on the Notion Press Platform
www.notionpress.com

DEDICATION

To those who dare to dream, strive for greatness, and embrace the power of their own potential.

Contents

Contents

Prayer

"Om Poornamadah Poornamidam Poornaat Poornamudachyate, Poornasya Poornamaadaya Poornamevavashishyate"

"Om Shantih, Shantih, Shantih"

The literal interpretation of this mantra is: That which is Absolute, This which is Absolute, Absolute arises from Absolute, If Absolute is removed from Absolute, Absolute remains

This mantra is a reminder of the fundamental truth that all of existence is rooted in the Absolute. It is a reminder that the Absolute is the source of all that is, and that it is ever-present, even when all else is taken away. It is a reminder of the peace that comes from understanding and accepting this truth.

Om Peace, Peace, Peace.

About The Author

Dr. Minakshi Bansal, born in the bustling metropolis of Delhi, India, has led a life steeped in artistry, scholarly pursuit, and an unwavering commitment to societal betterment. Following her marriage, she relocated to Ahmedabad, Gujarat, where she has since blossomed into a multifaceted beacon of inspiration for many. Dr. Minakshi is not only recognized as a gifted artist in the realm of Fine Arts but also as an esteemed author, a devoted social worker and a dedicated research scholar in Psychology. Her journey, marked by a profound dedication to elevating those around her, especially the downtrodden and underprivileged children of society, is a testament to her deep-seated belief in the transformative power of engagement and empathy.

From her earliest days, Minakshi was distinguished by an insatiable appetite for reading. Her literary universe was inhabited by characters and narratives that spanned ethical tales, motivational and inspirational stories, and the mythic parables imbued with life lessons. This voracious reading habit was not merely for personal edification but was driven by a desire to distill and disseminate the essence of these narratives to foster the development of students and peers alike. She was particularly captivated by the lives and teachings of historical figures and spiritual leaders such as Adi Shankaracharya, Swami Vivekananda, Dr. APJ Abdul Kalam, Mahamana Pandit Madan Mohan Malviya, Mahatma Gandhi, Sardar Vallabhai Patel, and Vinoba Bhave, among others. Their philosophies and life stories fueled her ambition to embody their ideals of resilience, selflessness, and relentless pursuit of knowledge.

Dr. Minakshi's academic and practical engagement with psychology has been equally noteworthy. As a research scholar, her focus has been on exploring the intricate tapestry of the human psyche, aiming to unlock the potential for psychological well-being and societal harmony. Her scholarly work is complemented by her active involvement in social work, where she employs her academic insights to make tangible differences in the lives of the underprivileged. Her endeavours in social work are characterized by an innovative approach that combines traditional wisdom with contemporary psychological practices to address the multifaceted challenges faced by these communities.

Her artistic talents, another facet of her diverse capabilities, are not merely a personal passion but also serve as a medium through which she communicates and connects with others. Her art, rich in symbolism and emotional depth, reflects her philosophical inquiries and social concerns, offering viewers a glimpse into the breadth of her intellect and the depth of her compassion.

In addition to her contributions to the arts and social sciences, Dr. Minakshi has embraced the healing arts of Pranic Healing, mastering the techniques developed by Master Choa Kok Sui. This practice, which focuses on the manipulation of Prana or life energy to heal the body and aura, has been both a personal journey of discovery and a means through which she extends her healing touch to others. Her proficiency in Pranic Healing is complemented by her advocacy and teaching of various forms of meditation aimed at rejuvenation, personal betterment, and the cultivation of harmony within individuals and communities alike.

Dr. Minakshi's life is a narrative of relentless pursuit, not just of personal achievement but of the upliftment and empowerment of society at large. Her diverse interests and talents—spanning the arts, literature, psychology, and the healing practices—converge on a singular path of service. She embodies the spirit of the luminaries who inspired her, channelling their legacy through her actions and teachings. Through her books, art, and social initiatives, she continues to inspire a new generation to embark on their own journeys of self-discovery, resilience, and altruism.

Her commitment to social betterment, particularly her focus on uplifting underprivileged children, reflects a deep understanding of the transformative potential of education and personal development. By integrating her knowledge of psychology, her artistic sensibilities, and her healing practices, Dr. Bansal has developed a holistic approach to social work that addresses both the immediate needs and the long-term well-being of the communities she serves.

As an author, Dr. Minakshi's writings offer a blend of inspirational insights, practical wisdom, and reflective contemplations drawn from her extensive reading and life experiences. Her books serve as a guide for those seeking to navigate the complexities of life with grace, resilience, and purpose. Through her narratives, she extends an invitation to her readers to explore the depths of their own potential and to contribute meaningfully to the collective well-being of society.

In Dr. Minakshi Bansal, we find a remarkable synthesis of the artist, the scholar, the healer, and the social activist. Her life's work stands as a beacon of hope and a source of inspiration for individuals seeking to make a difference in the world. Her story is a compelling reminder of the power of individual action, rooted in compassion and driven by a profound commitment to the betterment of humanity. Dr. Minakshi's legacy is not just in the tangible outcomes of her efforts but in the enduring spirit of inquiry, empathy, and service that she embodies.

Preface

In the tapestry of life, the threads of proactivity and productivity intertwine to create a masterpiece of achievement and fulfillment. As I embarked on my own journey towards personal and professional growth, I became increasingly fascinated by the power of habits, those seemingly small actions that, when repeated consistently, can have a profound impact on our lives. Through years of research, experimentation, and self-reflection, I discovered a set of principles and practices that have not only transformed my own life but have also helped countless others achieve their goals and aspirations.

In this book, I share these principles and practices with you, offering a blueprint for crafting habits that foster proactivity and productivity. This is not a one-size-fits-all approach, nor is it a quick fix. It is a journey of self-discovery, continuous learning, and deliberate practice. It requires a commitment to change, a willingness to step outside of our comfort zones, and a relentless pursuit of excellence.

The journey begins with a shift in mindset. We must embrace the power of proactivity, taking ownership of our lives and actively shaping our destinies. This involves setting clear and meaningful goals, developing effective time management strategies, and prioritizing tasks that align with our values and aspirations. It also requires us to overcome the insidious habit of procrastination, understanding its root causes and implementing strategies to counteract its detrimental effects.

As we progress on this journey, the importance of building a routine becomes apparent. A well-crafted routine provides a sense of structure and predictability, enabling us to focus our energy on what truly matters. It helps us establish healthy habits, overcome procrastination, and create more time for the activities we enjoy. A routine is not a rigid schedule, but rather a flexible framework that adapts to our individual needs and preferences.

Effective planning is another essential component of our journey. By outlining the specific steps, actions, and resources required to achieve our goals, we create a clear roadmap for success. Anticipating obstacles, continuously monitoring our progress, and leveraging technology can further enhance our planning efforts, ensuring that we stay on track and adapt to changing circumstances.

Along the way, we must not forget the importance of rest and recovery. In our relentless pursuit of productivity, we often neglect the vital role that rest plays in our physical, mental, and emotional well-being. By prioritizing rest and incorporating various forms of rejuvenation into our daily lives, we can recharge our batteries, improve our cognitive function, and enhance our overall performance.

To optimize our focus and productivity, we must also learn to minimize distractions. The modern world is rife with distractions, from the constant pings of notifications to the allure of social media. By setting boundaries, creating a distraction-free workspace, and managing both external and internal distractions, we can cultivate an environment conducive to deep work and meaningful engagement.

Leveraging technology is another key aspect of our journey. By utilizing digital tools and platforms, we can automate tasks, access vast repositories of information, foster collaboration, and stay abreast of the latest trends and developments. However, it is essential to strike a balance between embracing technology and maintaining our human connection, ensuring that we do not become overly reliant on digital tools.

Continuous learning is the lifeblood of personal and professional growth. By actively seeking out new knowledge, skills, and perspectives, we remain adaptable, innovative, and competitive in an ever-changing world. Formal education, informal learning, mentoring, and coaching are all valuable avenues for continuous learning, and the internet offers a wealth of resources for those who are eager to expand their horizons.

As we progress on our journey, celebrating our progress is crucial for maintaining motivation and building resilience. Acknowledging and appreciating our achievements, both big and small, reinforces positive behaviors, boosts our self-confidence, and fuels our drive to continue striving for success. By taking the time to celebrate our wins, we create a positive feedback loop that encourages us to persevere in the face of challenges.

Finally, adapting to change is an inevitable part of life. The world around us is in a constant state of flux, and our ability to adapt to these changes is essential for our survival and success. By cultivating a growth mindset, remaining flexible, embracing learning, and collaborating with others, we can navigate change with grace, resilience, and optimism.

This book is not a magic formula for success, but rather a guide to help you discover your own path to proactivity and productivity. It is a toolbox filled with practical strategies, insights, and inspiration to empower you to take charge of your life, achieve your goals, and live a more fulfilling and purposeful life.

I invite you to embark on this journey with an open mind and a willingness to experiment. The principles and practices outlined in this book are not meant to be followed rigidly, but rather adapted to your individual needs and circumstances. Remember, the journey of self-improvement is a lifelong one, and there is no single path to success. The most important thing is to start, to take that first step, and to never stop learning and growing.

Dr. Minakshi Bansal
Social Activist
Ahmedabad, Gujarat, Bharat

ONE
THE POWER OF PROACTIVITY

In the relentless pursuit of success, be it in the professional sphere or personal growth, the power of proactivity emerges as an undeniable force. Unlike reactivity, where individuals merely respond to external stimuli or circumstances, proactivity involves taking charge and initiating action. It is a mindset that empowers individuals to shape their own destinies, rather than being passive spectators in the theater of life. The proactive approach is characterized by initiative, foresight, and a relentless drive to improve oneself and one's surroundings. It is about not just reacting to events, but actively seeking opportunities and creating positive change.

At its core, proactivity is about taking responsibility for one's life. It is a conscious decision to stop blaming external factors for one's failures or shortcomings and instead focus on what one can control. This shift in perspective can be transformative. It allows individuals to break free from the shackles of victimhood and step into a position of empowerment. Proactive people understand that they are the architects of their own lives and that their choices and actions ultimately determine their outcomes.

One of the most significant advantages of proactivity is its ability to unlock a wealth of opportunities. By taking the initiative and actively seeking out new possibilities, individuals open themselves up to a world of growth and advancement. This can be particularly beneficial in the professional realm, where proactivity is often seen as a key trait of successful leaders and entrepreneurs. Those who are willing to step outside their comfort zones and take risks are often the ones who reap the greatest rewards.

Proactivity is also closely linked to personal development. By constantly seeking ways to improve themselves, proactive individuals are able to cultivate a wide range of skills and knowledge. This not only enhances their professional capabilities but also contributes to their overall well-being and happiness. The pursuit of personal growth is an ongoing journey, and proactivity is the fuel that keeps it moving forward.

Another crucial aspect of proactivity is its role in problem-solving. While reactive individuals may wait for problems to arise before taking action, proactive individuals actively seek out potential challenges and address them before they escalate. This ability to anticipate and mitigate problems can be invaluable in both personal and professional life. It allows individuals to stay one step ahead and avoid unnecessary setbacks.

Furthermore, proactivity is a powerful tool for building relationships and fostering collaboration. By taking the initiative to connect with others, offer help, and contribute to shared goals, proactive individuals are able to forge strong bonds with colleagues, friends, and family. This not only enriches their personal lives but also creates a network of support that can be invaluable in times of need.

In the face of adversity, proactivity shines as a beacon of hope. When faced with challenges, proactive individuals do not succumb to despair or helplessness. Instead, they view obstacles as opportunities for growth and learning. They approach problems with a solutions-oriented mindset, seeking ways to overcome difficulties and emerge stronger on the other side.

The power of proactivity is not confined to any particular domain. It is a universal principle that can be applied in all aspects of life. Whether it is striving for professional success, cultivating personal growth, building relationships, or overcoming challenges, proactivity provides a roadmap for achieving one's goals. It is a mindset that empowers individuals to take control of their lives, shape their destinies, and create a meaningful impact on the world around them.

Proactivity is the spark that ignites progress. It's not about waiting for opportunities, but about creating them. Embrace the power of taking initiative, and watch your life transform.

TWO

Setting Clear Goals

Setting clear goals is the cornerstone of any successful endeavor, be it personal or professional. Goals provide a sense of direction, purpose, and motivation. Without clear goals, it is easy to become adrift, wasting time and energy on activities that do not contribute to our overall objectives. Setting clear goals is not merely about wishing or dreaming; it is a deliberate and systematic process that involves defining what we want to achieve, why we want to achieve it, and how we plan to get there.

The first step in setting clear goals is to identify what we truly want to accomplish. This requires introspection and self-awareness. We need to delve deep into our desires, aspirations, and values to determine what truly matters to us. It is important to distinguish between wants and needs, between superficial desires and genuine aspirations. Once we have a clear understanding of our ultimate objectives, we can begin to formulate specific goals that align with those objectives.

The next step is to make our goals specific and measurable. Vague or ambiguous goals are difficult to pursue and even harder to achieve. A goal such as "I want to be successful" is too broad and lacks clarity.

Instead, we need to break down our goals into specific, actionable steps. For example, if our objective is to improve our fitness, a specific goal could be "I will run a 5K marathon in under 30 minutes within six months." This goal is specific, measurable, and provides a clear target to work towards.

In addition to being specific and measurable, goals should also be achievable and realistic. Setting unrealistic goals is a recipe for disappointment and disillusionment. While it is important to challenge ourselves, it is equally important to set goals that are within our reach. This does not mean aiming low; it means setting goals that are challenging yet attainable with effort and dedication. By setting realistic goals, we increase our chances of success and build momentum for future endeavors.

Another crucial aspect of setting clear goals is to establish a timeframe for their completion. Goals without deadlines are prone to procrastination and inertia. A deadline creates a sense of urgency and compels us to take action. It provides a clear target date by which we expect to achieve our goals. This helps us stay focused and motivated, as we can track our progress and make necessary adjustments along the way.

Once we have set our goals, it is important to write them down. The act of writing down our goals solidifies them in our minds and makes them more tangible. It also serves as a constant reminder of what we are working towards. Our written goals can be placed in a visible location, such as on our desk or refrigerator, where we can see them every day. This helps us stay focused and motivated, even when faced with challenges or setbacks.

Setting clear goals is not a one-time event; it is an ongoing process. As we progress towards our goals, we may need to make adjustments or even revise our goals altogether. Life is dynamic, and our circumstances may change. It is important to be flexible and adaptable, while still maintaining our focus on our ultimate objectives. Regularly reviewing our goals and making necessary adjustments ensures that we stay on track and continue to make progress.

Setting clear goals is a fundamental step towards achieving success in any area of life. It provides direction, purpose, and motivation. By identifying our true desires, formulating specific and measurable goals, setting realistic deadlines, writing down our goals, and regularly reviewing and adjusting them, we can significantly increase our chances of success. Clear goals are not just a roadmap to our destination; they are a compass that guides us through the journey of life. They empower us to take control of our destiny and create the life we truly desire.

Clear goals are the compass that guides your journey. They provide direction, purpose, and a measure of success. Define your destination, and then chart a course to reach it.

ᑭᑭᑭ

THREE

Time Management Techniques

Time, often described as the most valuable resource, is finite and irreplaceable. In the fast-paced and demanding world we live in, the effective management of time is not just a desirable skill; it's an absolute necessity. Time management is not about cramming as much as possible into a day, but rather about optimizing our time to achieve our goals and live a more fulfilling life. A multitude of time management techniques exist, each with its own strengths and applications, but all share the common goal of helping us make the most of our time.

One of the most fundamental time management techniques is prioritization. The Pareto Principle, also known as the 80/20 rule, states that roughly 80% of results come from 20% of efforts. Applying this principle to time management means identifying the most important tasks that will yield the greatest results and focusing our energy on those tasks. This requires the ability to distinguish between urgent and important tasks, and to resist the urge to get caught up in trivial matters.

Another essential technique is planning. Creating a to-do list or schedule can help us visualize our tasks and allocate time for each one. It's important to be realistic when planning and to allow for unexpected delays or interruptions. Breaking down large tasks into smaller, more manageable chunks can also make them seem less daunting and more achievable. Utilizing tools such as calendars, planners, or time management apps can further enhance our planning process.

The Pomodoro Technique is a popular time management method that involves working in focused bursts of 25 minutes, followed by a short break. This technique can help improve focus and productivity by breaking down work into manageable intervals and allowing for regular rest periods. The breaks can be used for physical activity, relaxation, or any other activity that helps clear the mind and recharge.

Another effective technique is timeboxing, which involves allocating a fixed amount of time for a specific task. This can help prevent tasks from dragging on indefinitely and ensure that we make progress on all our priorities. Timeboxing can be combined with other techniques, such as the Pomodoro Technique, for even greater efficiency. For example, we could timebox a task for two Pomodoro sessions, with a longer break in between.

Delegation is another powerful time management tool. We don't have to do everything ourselves; often, we can delegate tasks to others who are better equipped or have more time to handle them. This frees up our time to focus on our core responsibilities and priorities. Delegation requires trust and clear communication, but it can be a game-changer for those who struggle with overcommitment.

Avoiding multitasking is another key to effective time management. Contrary to popular belief, multitasking does not save time; it actually hinders productivity. When we try to do multiple things at once, our attention is divided, and we end up taking longer to complete each task. Focusing on one task at a time allows us to give it our full attention and complete it more efficiently.

In addition to these techniques, there are several other strategies that can help us manage our time more effectively. These include:

Setting boundaries: Learning to say no to requests that are not aligned with our priorities is essential for protecting our time and energy.

Minimizing distractions: Eliminating or reducing distractions, such as notifications, social media, or unnecessary meetings, can significantly improve focus and productivity.

Batching tasks: Grouping similar tasks together, such as checking emails or making phone calls, can save time by eliminating the need to switch gears constantly.

Automating tasks: Utilizing technology to automate repetitive tasks, such as bill payments or social media scheduling, can free up time for more important activities.

Effective time management is an ongoing process that requires self-awareness, discipline, and a willingness to experiment with different techniques. By applying the strategies outlined above and continuously refining our approach, we can reclaim control of our time and achieve our goals with greater ease and efficiency. Remember, time is a gift, and how we choose to use it is ultimately up to us.

Time is your most precious asset. Invest it wisely in activities that align with your goals and values. Prioritize what truly matters, and let go of what doesn't serve you.

♡♡♡

FOUR

Prioritization Strategies

In the ceaseless flow of tasks and responsibilities that characterize modern life, the ability to prioritize effectively stands as a cornerstone of productivity and success. Prioritization is the art and science of determining which tasks deserve our immediate attention and which can be deferred or delegated. It is a skill that enables us to navigate the complexities of our daily lives, both personal and professional, with greater efficiency and focus.

At its core, prioritization is about making conscious choices about how we allocate our time and energy. It is about recognizing that not all tasks are created equal and that some will have a greater impact on our goals and well-being than others. Effective prioritization requires us to step back from the daily whirlwind and assess our tasks objectively, considering their urgency, importance, and potential consequences.

One of the most widely used prioritization strategies is the Eisenhower Matrix, named after former US President Dwight D. Eisenhower. This matrix categorizes tasks into four quadrants based on their urgency and importance. Quadrant I contains tasks that are both urgent and important, such as crises or deadlines.

Quadrant II contains tasks that are important but not urgent, such as long-term goals or relationship building. Quadrant III contains tasks that are urgent but not important, such as interruptions or some meetings. Quadrant IV contains tasks that are neither urgent nor important, such as busywork or time-wasters. The Eisenhower Matrix encourages us to focus on Quadrant II activities, as these are the ones that contribute most to our long-term success and well-being.

Another popular prioritization method is the ABCDE method, which involves assigning a letter to each task based on its priority. A tasks are the most important and must be done immediately. B tasks are important but not as urgent as A tasks. C tasks are nice to have but not essential. D tasks can be delegated to others. E tasks can be eliminated altogether. By categorizing tasks in this way, we can quickly identify which ones deserve our immediate attention and which can be deferred or delegated.

The MoSCoW method is another useful prioritization framework, particularly in project management. It stands for Must Have, Should Have, Could Have, and Won't Have. Must Have tasks are essential for the project's success and must be completed. Should Have tasks are important but not critical, and their completion would add value to the project. Could Have tasks are desirable but not essential, and their completion would be a bonus. Won't Have tasks are those that will not be included in the current project but may be considered for future iterations.

In addition to these formal frameworks, there are several other prioritization strategies that can be effective. One such strategy is to consider the impact of a task. Will completing this task have a significant impact on my goals? If so, it should be given higher priority. Another strategy is to consider the effort required to complete a task. Is this task something I can do quickly and easily, or will it require a significant investment of time and energy? Tasks that require less effort may be good candidates for quick wins, while those that require more effort may need to be broken down into smaller, more manageable steps.

The ability to prioritize effectively is not a static skill; it is a dynamic process that requires ongoing refinement. As our lives and circumstances change, so too must our priorities. It is important to regularly review and reassess our tasks, considering their relevance to our current goals and circumstances. This allows us to adapt to changing priorities and ensure that we are always focusing on the most important tasks at hand.

Ultimately, prioritization is about taking control of our time and energy and directing it towards what truly matters. It is about making conscious choices about how we spend our days, rather than simply reacting to whatever comes our way. By mastering the art of prioritization, we can increase our productivity, achieve our goals, and live more fulfilling lives.

PPP

Procrastination is a thief of time and potential. Break free from its grip by understanding your triggers and implementing strategies for overcoming it. Remember, the best time to start is now.

ჾჾჾ

FIVE

BUILDING A ROUTINE

The art of building a routine is akin to constructing a sturdy framework for a productive and fulfilling life. A routine is not a rigid, inflexible schedule, but rather a structured sequence of activities that create rhythm and predictability in our daily lives. It is a powerful tool that can enhance our focus, productivity, and overall well-being. By establishing a routine, we create a sense of order and control amidst the chaos of modern life, enabling us to channel our energy towards our goals and aspirations.

The foundation of any routine is consistency. A routine only becomes effective when it is practiced regularly and consistently. This does not mean that every day must be identical, but rather that there are certain core activities that are performed at roughly the same time each day. This consistency creates a sense of familiarity and predictability, which can reduce anxiety and stress. It also helps to establish healthy habits and patterns of behavior.

One of the key benefits of having a routine is that it reduces decision fatigue. When we have a set routine, we don't have to constantly make decisions about what to do next or when to do it. This frees up mental energy that can be used for more important tasks. For example, if we have a set time for exercise each day, we don't have to waste time debating whether or not to go to the gym. We simply follow our routine, and the decision is already made for us.

Another advantage of a routine is that it can help us overcome procrastination. When we have a structured schedule, it becomes easier to get started on tasks, even when we don't feel like it. The routine itself provides a sense of momentum and helps us overcome inertia. For example, if we have a set time for writing each day, we are more likely to sit down and start writing, even if we initially feel uninspired.

A routine can also help us improve our sleep quality. By going to bed and waking up at the same time each day, we regulate our circadian rhythm, which is our body's natural sleep-wake cycle. This can lead to deeper, more restful sleep, which in turn improves our energy levels, focus, and overall well-being. A consistent sleep schedule can also help alleviate insomnia and other sleep disorders.

In addition to these benefits, a routine can also help us create more time for the things we enjoy. By scheduling our work and other obligations, we free up time for hobbies, leisure activities, and social interactions. This can lead to a more balanced and fulfilling life, as we are not solely focused on work or other responsibilities. A routine can also help us make time for self-care activities, such as exercise, meditation, or spending time in nature.

Building a routine requires intentionality and self-discipline. It is not something that happens overnight, but rather a gradual process that involves experimentation and adjustment. The first step is to identify the core activities that are most important to us, such as work, exercise, sleep, and leisure. We then need to determine the optimal time for each activity, based on our individual preferences and energy levels. Once we have established a basic framework, we can start to experiment with different variations and adjust our routine as needed.

It is important to note that a routine is not a one-size-fits-all solution. What works for one person may not work for another. The key is to find a routine that fits our individual needs and lifestyles. Some people may prefer a highly structured routine with set times for every activity, while others may prefer a more flexible routine with room for spontaneity. The most important thing is to find a routine that works for us and helps us achieve our goals.

Building a routine is a powerful tool for enhancing productivity, focus, and overall well-being. By establishing a structured sequence of activities, we create a sense of order and control in our lives. A routine can help us reduce decision fatigue, overcome procrastination, improve our sleep quality, and create more time for the things we enjoy. Building a routine requires intentionality and self-discipline, but the rewards are well worth the effort.

Your mindset is the key to unlocking your full potential. Embrace a growth mindset, believe in your ability to learn and improve, and watch yourself soar to new heights.

ღღღ

SIX

OVERCOMING PROCRASTINATION

Procrastination, the act of delaying or postponing a task or set of tasks, is a common human experience that affects people from all walks of life. It is a pervasive and often debilitating habit that can hinder personal growth, impede professional success, and create unnecessary stress and anxiety. Overcoming procrastination is a multifaceted challenge that requires a deep understanding of its root causes, as well as the implementation of effective strategies to counteract its detrimental effects.

At its core, procrastination is not simply about laziness or a lack of willpower. It is a complex psychological phenomenon that stems from a variety of factors, including fear of failure, perfectionism, lack of motivation, poor time management skills, and difficulty concentrating. By understanding the underlying causes of our procrastination, we can begin to develop tailored strategies to address them.

One of the most effective ways to overcome procrastination is to break down large, overwhelming tasks into smaller, more manageable ones. This approach can make the task seem less daunting and more achievable, reducing the likelihood of procrastination. Additionally, setting realistic deadlines and creating a schedule can help us stay on track and avoid last-minute rushes.

Another key strategy is to identify our personal procrastination triggers. These are the specific situations or circumstances that tend to lead us to procrastinate. For some, it might be the fear of starting a difficult task, while for others, it might be the temptation of distractions like social media or television. Once we are aware of our triggers, we can take steps to avoid or minimize them. For example, if we know that we tend to procrastinate when working in a noisy environment, we can try to find a quieter place to work or use noise-canceling headphones.

Rewarding ourselves for completing tasks can also be a powerful motivator in overcoming procrastination. This can involve anything from enjoying a favorite treat to taking a break to do something we enjoy. By associating task completion with positive reinforcement, we can create a positive feedback loop that encourages us to stay on track.

Sometimes, procrastination can stem from a lack of clarity or understanding about a task. In such cases, seeking clarification or additional information can be helpful. Talking to a colleague, mentor, or friend can provide us with the necessary guidance and support to get started. Additionally, breaking down the task into smaller steps and identifying the first actionable step can make it easier to overcome the initial inertia.

It is important to recognize that overcoming procrastination is not a one-size-fits-all endeavor. What works for one person may not work for another. It may require experimentation with different strategies to find what works best for us. Additionally, it is important to be patient and kind to ourselves. Overcoming procrastination is a process that takes time and effort, and setbacks are a natural part of the journey.

Procrastination is a common but surmountable challenge. By understanding its root causes, identifying our personal triggers, breaking down tasks into smaller steps, setting deadlines, rewarding ourselves, seeking clarification when needed, and experimenting with different strategies, we can overcome procrastination and achieve our goals. Remember, the key is to start, even if it is with a small step. Progress, no matter how small, is still progress. With persistence and dedication, we can break free from the shackles of procrastination and unlock our full potential.

ppp

A routine is the backbone of productivity. Establish consistent habits that support your goals and values, and watch your life transform into a symphony of achievement.

SEVEN

The Role of Mindset

The role of mindset in achieving success and personal fulfillment is a subject that has garnered significant attention in recent years. While external factors like resources, opportunities, and even luck undoubtedly play a role, the internal landscape of our minds holds a profound influence on our outcomes. Mindset, often defined as a set of beliefs and attitudes that shape how we perceive ourselves and the world around us, can be a powerful determinant of our actions, behaviors, and ultimately, our achievements.

At the heart of this discussion lies the distinction between fixed and growth mindsets, a concept popularized by psychologist Carol Dweck. A fixed mindset is characterized by the belief that our abilities and intelligence are static and unchangeable. Individuals with a fixed mindset tend to avoid challenges, fearing failure as a reflection of their inherent limitations. They may also shy away from feedback, viewing it as a critique of their fixed capabilities.

In contrast, a growth mindset embraces the idea that our abilities can be developed through dedication and hard work. People with a growth mindset see challenges as opportunities for learning and growth, and they embrace feedback as a means of improvement.

They are not afraid to put in the effort required to achieve their goals, as they believe that their abilities are not fixed but can be cultivated over time.

The implications of these differing mindsets are far-reaching. A fixed mindset can lead to a fear of failure, a reluctance to take risks, and a tendency to give up easily in the face of setbacks. On the other hand, a growth mindset fosters resilience, a willingness to embrace challenges, and a persistent pursuit of improvement. It is this growth mindset that is often associated with high achievers and individuals who consistently reach their full potential.

The power of mindset extends beyond individual achievement. It can also shape our relationships, our careers, and even our overall happiness and well-being. A growth mindset fosters a love of learning, a curiosity about the world, and a willingness to collaborate with others. It allows us to see setbacks as temporary and to view criticism as an opportunity for growth. In contrast, a fixed mindset can lead to defensiveness, resentment, and a fear of vulnerability.

Cultivating a growth mindset is not an overnight process, but it is a worthwhile endeavor. It involves challenging our limiting beliefs, reframing our self-talk, and embracing a lifelong journey of learning and development. It means recognizing that our potential is not fixed but can be expanded through effort and perseverance.

One practical way to foster a growth mindset is to focus on the process of learning rather than solely on the outcome. When we prioritize learning, we are more likely to embrace challenges and setbacks as opportunities for growth. We can also cultivate a growth mindset by seeking out feedback, both positive and negative, as a means of identifying areas for improvement.

Additionally, surrounding ourselves with positive and supportive individuals can play a crucial role in developing a growth mindset. When we are surrounded by people who believe in our ability to grow and improve, we are more likely to believe in ourselves.

The role of mindset in shaping our lives is undeniable. A fixed mindset can limit our potential and hold us back from achieving our goals, while a growth mindset can empower us to overcome challenges, embrace learning, and reach our full potential. By understanding the difference between these two mindsets and actively cultivating a growth mindset, we can unlock a world of possibilities and create a more fulfilling and successful life.

Effective planning is the roadmap to success. Chart your course, anticipate obstacles, and adapt to changing circumstances. With a well-crafted plan, you can conquer any challenge.

♡♡♡

EIGHT

DEVELOPING SELF-DISCIPLINE

Self-discipline, often described as the ability to control one's impulses and actions in pursuit of long-term goals, is a cornerstone of personal and professional success. It is the force that allows us to resist temptations, overcome obstacles, and persevere in the face of adversity. Developing self-discipline is not an overnight process, but rather a lifelong journey that requires commitment, perseverance, and a willingness to confront our weaknesses.

At its core, self-discipline is about making choices that align with our values and goals, even when those choices are difficult or uncomfortable. It is about delaying gratification in the present for the sake of greater rewards in the future. For example, a student who chooses to study for an exam instead of going out with friends is exercising self-discipline. Similarly, an athlete who sticks to a rigorous training regimen, even when tired or discouraged, is demonstrating self-discipline.

The importance of self-discipline cannot be overstated. It is a key factor in achieving success in virtually every area of life. In the academic realm, self-discipline is essential for maintaining focus, completing assignments on time, and achieving academic goals. In the professional world, it is crucial for meeting deadlines, managing workloads, and building a successful career. In personal relationships, self-discipline helps us to be reliable, trustworthy, and considerate of others.

Developing self-discipline is a multifaceted process that involves various strategies and techniques. One of the most fundamental steps is to set clear, specific goals. Without a clear target in mind, it is easy to lose focus and succumb to distractions. Our goals should be challenging yet achievable, and we should break them down into smaller, more manageable steps. This will help us track our progress and stay motivated.

Another key element of self-discipline is creating a routine. A consistent routine provides structure and predictability, which can help us stay on track and avoid impulsive decisions. It is important to schedule time for the activities that are most important to us, such as work, exercise, and spending time with loved ones. A routine also helps us establish healthy habits, such as getting enough sleep, eating nutritious meals, and exercising regularly.

To cultivate self-discipline, it is also crucial to manage our environment. This means minimizing distractions and creating a space that is conducive to focus and productivity. For example, if we are trying to study, we might turn off our phone, close our email, and find a quiet place to work. Similarly, if we are trying to eat healthier, we might stock our refrigerator with nutritious foods and avoid keeping junk food in the house.

Overcoming temptations is another critical aspect of self-discipline. We all face temptations, whether it's the urge to procrastinate, indulge in unhealthy habits, or give up on our goals. The key is to develop strategies for resisting these temptations. This might involve finding healthy alternatives, such as going for a walk instead of reaching for a sugary snack, or reminding ourselves of the long-term benefits of staying on track.

Self-discipline is not about being perfect. We all slip up from time to time. The important thing is to learn from our mistakes and get back on track as quickly as possible. By practicing self-compassion and recognizing that setbacks are a natural part of the process, we can avoid getting discouraged and stay committed to our goals.

Developing self-discipline is a lifelong journey, but the rewards are immeasurable. It empowers us to achieve our dreams, live healthier lives, and build stronger relationships. It gives us the ability to control our impulses and make choices that align with our values and goals. By cultivating self-discipline, we unlock our full potential and create a life that is both fulfilling and meaningful.

Rest is not a luxury; it's a necessity. Recharge your body, mind, and spirit with regular breaks, restful sleep, and leisure activities. A well-rested you is a more productive and creative you.

ღღღ

NINE

Effective Planning

Effective planning is the linchpin of success in any endeavor, be it personal, professional, or organizational. It is a dynamic process that involves setting clear goals, outlining a roadmap to achieve those goals, and continuously adapting to changing circumstances. A well-crafted plan not only provides a sense of direction but also acts as a compass, guiding us through the turbulent waters of uncertainty and ensuring that we stay on course towards our desired destination.

At its core, effective planning begins with a clear understanding of our objectives. What do we want to achieve? What are our priorities? What are the desired outcomes? By articulating our goals with precision, we lay the groundwork for a focused and purposeful plan. This initial step requires introspection and a thorough assessment of our values, aspirations, and resources.

Once our goals are defined, the next step is to develop a comprehensive strategy. This involves outlining the specific steps, actions, and resources required to achieve our objectives. It is essential to break down complex goals into smaller, more manageable tasks, as this makes them seem less daunting and more achievable. Each task should have a clearly defined timeline, ensuring that we stay on track and make steady progress.

A crucial aspect of effective planning is the ability to anticipate potential obstacles and develop contingency plans. No plan is foolproof, and unforeseen challenges are bound to arise. By identifying potential risks and devising strategies to mitigate them, we can minimize the impact of these challenges and avoid derailment. This requires a proactive approach, where we constantly assess our environment and adjust our plans accordingly.

Effective planning also involves regular monitoring and evaluation. It is not enough to simply create a plan and set it in motion. We must continuously track our progress, assess our performance, and make adjustments as needed. This feedback loop allows us to identify what is working well and what needs improvement, ensuring that our plan remains relevant and effective.

The use of technology can significantly enhance the planning process. A plethora of tools and applications are available to help us organize our tasks, track our progress, and collaborate with others. Project management software, calendar apps, and note-taking tools can all be invaluable assets in streamlining our planning efforts and maximizing our productivity.

Furthermore, effective planning is not a solitary endeavor. It often involves collaboration and communication with others. Whether it is seeking input from colleagues, delegating tasks, or seeking guidance from mentors, working with others can enrich our perspectives and enhance the quality of our plans. Effective communication ensures that everyone involved understands their roles and responsibilities, contributing to a smoother and more efficient execution of the plan.

Another crucial element of effective planning is flexibility. While it is important to have a clear roadmap, we must also be adaptable and willing to adjust our plans as needed. The world is constantly changing, and our plans must evolve with it. By embracing change and remaining flexible, we can ensure that our plans remain relevant and effective in the face of new challenges and opportunities.

Finally, effective planning is not just about achieving goals; it is also about personal growth and development. Through the process of planning, we learn about ourselves, our strengths, our weaknesses, and our values. We develop critical thinking skills, problem-solving abilities, and decision-making capabilities. The discipline and focus required for effective planning can spill over into other areas of our lives, leading to greater personal fulfillment and overall success.

Effective planning is an indispensable tool for achieving our goals and aspirations. By setting clear objectives, developing comprehensive strategies, anticipating obstacles, monitoring our progress, leveraging technology, collaborating with others, and remaining flexible, we can navigate the complexities of life with greater confidence and purpose. Effective planning is not merely about getting things done; it is about creating a meaningful and fulfilling life.

Distractions are the enemy of focus. Minimize them by creating a distraction-free environment, setting boundaries, and prioritizing deep work. Protect your attention, and your productivity will soar.

TEN

Breaking Down Goals

In the pursuit of ambitious goals, whether they be personal, professional, or organizational, the path to success is often paved with challenges and obstacles. These challenges can seem insurmountable, leading to frustration, demotivation, and even abandonment of the goal altogether. However, there is a powerful strategy that can transform daunting goals into achievable milestones: breaking them down into smaller, more manageable tasks.

The process of breaking down goals is akin to dismantling a complex puzzle into its individual pieces. By deconstructing a large, overarching goal into smaller, bite-sized tasks, we create a clear roadmap that outlines the specific steps required to reach our destination. This approach not only makes the goal seem less intimidating but also provides a sense of progress and accomplishment as each task is completed.

One of the key benefits of breaking down goals is that it helps to overcome the feeling of overwhelm that often accompanies ambitious endeavors. When faced with a monumental task, it is easy to feel paralyzed by its sheer magnitude. However, by focusing on smaller, more achievable tasks, we shift our attention from the overwhelming whole to the manageable parts. This shift in perspective can be incredibly empowering, as it allows us to see the goal as a series of interconnected steps rather than a monolithic obstacle.

Breaking down goals also enables us to identify the specific skills, resources, and knowledge required to achieve each task. This allows us to allocate our time and energy more efficiently, ensuring that we are focusing on the most critical aspects of the goal. By identifying potential bottlenecks or areas where we lack expertise, we can proactively seek out solutions or support, increasing our chances of success.

Another advantage of this approach is that it provides a sense of progress and momentum. As we complete each task, we experience a sense of accomplishment and satisfaction, which fuels our motivation to continue. This positive feedback loop can be especially beneficial for long-term goals, where the finish line may seem distant and elusive. By celebrating small victories along the way, we maintain our enthusiasm and commitment to the larger objective.

Furthermore, breaking down goals allows for greater flexibility and adaptability. In the course of pursuing any goal, unforeseen challenges and opportunities are bound to arise. By having a granular plan with smaller tasks, we can more easily adjust our approach to accommodate these changes. This flexibility is crucial for navigating the unpredictable nature of life and ensuring that our goals remain relevant and achievable.

The process of breaking down goals can be approached in various ways. One common method is to create a hierarchical structure, where the main goal is divided into several sub-goals, each of which is further broken down into specific tasks. Another approach is to use a timeline, where tasks are assigned to specific dates or time periods. Regardless of the method used, the key is to create a plan that is detailed, realistic, and flexible.

Breaking down goals is a powerful strategy for achieving success in any endeavor. By deconstructing large, complex goals into smaller, more manageable tasks, we can overcome the feeling of overwhelm, identify specific requirements, build momentum, and adapt to changing circumstances. This approach not only increases our chances of success but also makes the journey towards our goals more enjoyable and fulfilling. Whether we are striving for personal growth, professional advancement, or organizational success, the ability to break down goals is an essential skill that can empower us to reach our full potential.

Technology is a powerful tool, but it's only as effective as the person wielding it. Leverage technology to enhance your efficiency, access information, and foster collaboration, but remember to maintain your human connection.

♡♡♡

ELEVEN

THE IMPORTANCE OF REST

In the relentless pursuit of productivity and achievement, the importance of rest often takes a back seat. We tend to glorify busyness and equate it with success, pushing ourselves to the limit in the belief that more work will inevitably lead to better results. However, this relentless pursuit of productivity often comes at a cost, as we neglect the vital role that rest plays in our physical, mental, and emotional well-being.

Rest is not merely the absence of activity; it is a multifaceted concept that encompasses various forms of rejuvenation. It includes sleep, relaxation, leisure activities, and even moments of stillness and contemplation. Each of these forms of rest serves a unique purpose, contributing to our overall health and well-being in different ways.

Sleep, often considered the cornerstone of rest, is essential for the body's repair and restoration processes. During sleep, our bodies undergo a series of physiological changes that are crucial for maintaining optimal health. These changes include the release of growth hormones, the repair of tissues, and the consolidation of memories. When we are sleep-deprived, these processes are disrupted, leading to a host of negative consequences, such as fatigue, impaired cognitive function, weakened immune system, and increased risk of chronic diseases.

Relaxation, another form of rest, involves reducing physical and mental tension. It can be achieved through various activities, such as meditation, deep breathing exercises, yoga, or simply taking a break from our daily routines. Relaxation helps to calm the nervous system, lower blood pressure, and reduce stress hormones. It also allows us to recharge our batteries and return to our tasks with renewed energy and focus.

Leisure activities, such as hobbies, sports, or spending time with loved ones, are also important forms of rest. They provide us with an opportunity to disconnect from work and other obligations, allowing us to recharge and de-stress. Engaging in activities we enjoy releases endorphins, the body's natural feel-good chemicals, which can boost our mood and overall well-being.

Moments of stillness and contemplation, often overlooked in our fast-paced lives, are also essential for rest. These moments allow us to reflect on our experiences, connect with our inner selves, and gain clarity on our thoughts and emotions. They can be as simple as taking a few minutes to sit quietly and observe our surroundings, or as involved as engaging in mindfulness meditation or journaling.

The benefits of rest are not limited to the physical and mental realms. Rest also plays a crucial role in our emotional well-being. When we are well-rested, we are better equipped to manage our emotions, cope with stress, and maintain healthy relationships. Conversely, lack of rest can lead to irritability, mood swings, and difficulty regulating our emotions.

In the professional sphere, the importance of rest is often underestimated. We tend to believe that working longer hours will lead to greater productivity, but research has shown that the opposite is often true. When we are overworked and sleep-deprived, our cognitive function suffers, leading to decreased productivity, increased errors, and poor decision-making. Taking regular breaks and ensuring adequate sleep can actually enhance our productivity and creativity.

Rest is not a luxury; it is a necessity. It is essential for our physical, mental, and emotional well-being. By prioritizing rest and incorporating various forms of rejuvenation into our daily lives, we can improve our health, enhance our productivity, and live more fulfilling lives. Rest is not a sign of weakness or laziness; it is a sign of self-awareness and a commitment to our overall well-being.

Continuous learning is the key to staying relevant and competitive in an ever-changing world. Embrace a growth mindset, seek out new knowledge and skills, and never stop learning.

TWELVE

MINIMIZING DISTRACTIONS

In our modern, hyper-connected world, distractions are ubiquitous. From the constant ping of notifications to the allure of social media, our attention is constantly being pulled in a multitude of directions. While some distractions may seem harmless, their cumulative effect can be significant, hindering our productivity, focus, and overall well-being. Minimizing distractions is not merely about eliminating all sources of interruption but rather about creating an environment that fosters concentration and allows us to engage fully in the task at hand.

One of the most pervasive distractions in today's world is technology. Our smartphones, tablets, and computers, while undoubtedly powerful tools, can also be major sources of distraction. The constant stream of notifications, emails, and social media updates can easily derail our focus and lead us down unproductive rabbit holes. To minimize technological distractions, we can adopt various strategies. One approach is to set specific times for checking emails and social media, rather than constantly reacting to notifications. We can also use apps and browser extensions that block distracting websites or limit our time on social media platforms. Additionally, silencing notifications or putting our devices on "Do Not Disturb" mode during focused work sessions can significantly reduce interruptions.

Another major source of distraction is our physical environment. A cluttered workspace, a noisy environment, or uncomfortable furniture can all hinder our ability to concentrate. To create a distraction-free workspace, we can declutter our desks, organize our materials, and ensure that we have adequate lighting and ventilation. If noise is a problem, we can use noise-canceling headphones or listen to calming music. Investing in ergonomic furniture can also improve our comfort and posture, reducing physical distractions.

Internal distractions, such as worries, anxieties, and daydreams, can also derail our focus. While it is impossible to completely eliminate these internal distractions, we can learn to manage them more effectively. Mindfulness meditation, deep breathing exercises, and other relaxation techniques can help us calm our minds and reduce the frequency and intensity of these internal distractions. Additionally, taking short breaks throughout the day can help us recharge and refocus, preventing mental fatigue and burnout.

Another effective strategy for minimizing distractions is to create a schedule and stick to it. By allocating specific time slots for different tasks, we can create a sense of structure and predictability in our day. This helps us stay on track and avoid getting sidetracked by less important activities. Additionally, by scheduling breaks and leisure time, we ensure that we are not overworking ourselves and that we have time for rest and relaxation.

Social distractions, such as conversations with colleagues or family members, can also be a major source of interruption. While social interaction is important, it can also be a significant distraction when we are trying to focus on a task. Setting boundaries and communicating our need for uninterrupted time can help minimize these social distractions. For example, we can close our office door, put up a "Do Not Disturb" sign, or let others know that we are not available for conversation at certain times.

Finally, it is important to recognize that minimizing distractions is an ongoing process. It requires constant vigilance and a willingness to adapt our strategies as needed. What works for one person may not work for another, so it is important to experiment with different techniques and find what works best for us. By cultivating a distraction-free environment, both externally and internally, we can unlock our full potential for focus, productivity, and creativity.

Celebrating progress fuels motivation and resilience. Acknowledge your achievements, both big and small, and take pride in the journey you've traveled. Each step forward is a victory worth celebrating.

♡♡♡

THIRTEEN

Leveraging Technology

In the modern era, technology has become an integral part of our daily lives, permeating every aspect of our existence. It has revolutionized the way we work, communicate, learn, and interact with the world around us. The advent of sophisticated tools and applications has empowered us to accomplish tasks that were once considered impossible, opening up a realm of possibilities that were previously unimaginable. Leveraging technology effectively is no longer a luxury but a necessity for individuals and organizations seeking to thrive in this digital age.

At its core, leveraging technology is about utilizing the power of digital tools and platforms to enhance our efficiency, productivity, and overall performance. It is about harnessing the capabilities of technology to streamline processes, automate repetitive tasks, and gain access to information and resources that were previously out of reach. This involves not only adopting the latest gadgets and software but also understanding how to integrate them seamlessly into our workflows and daily routines.

One of the most significant advantages of leveraging technology is its ability to automate mundane and repetitive tasks. By automating tasks such as data entry, scheduling, and report generation, we free up valuable time and mental energy that can be redirected towards more strategic and creative endeavors. This not only enhances our productivity but also reduces the risk of errors and improves the overall quality of our work.

Moreover, technology has democratized access to information and resources. With the advent of the internet and the proliferation of online platforms, we now have a wealth of knowledge at our fingertips. We can access online courses, tutorials, and research papers on virtually any topic imaginable, enabling us to learn new skills, expand our knowledge base, and stay ahead of the curve in our respective fields.

Technology has also revolutionized communication and collaboration. We can now connect with people from all over the world in real-time, transcending geographical boundaries and fostering global collaboration. Tools such as video conferencing, instant messaging, and project management software have made it easier than ever to collaborate with colleagues, clients, and partners, regardless of their location.

In the business world, leveraging technology is essential for staying competitive. Businesses that embrace digital transformation and leverage technology effectively are able to streamline their operations, improve their customer service, and gain a competitive edge in the marketplace. They can utilize data analytics to gain insights into customer behavior, optimize their marketing strategies, and make informed business decisions.

However, leveraging technology is not without its challenges. The rapid pace of technological advancement can make it difficult to keep up with the latest trends and tools. Moreover, there is a risk of becoming overly reliant on technology, leading to a loss of critical thinking skills and a decrease in face-to-face interaction. It is therefore essential to strike a balance between embracing technology and maintaining our human connection.

To leverage technology effectively, it is crucial to have a clear understanding of our goals and objectives. We need to identify the specific tasks and processes that can be enhanced through the use of technology and select the appropriate tools and platforms that align with our needs. It is also important to invest in training and development to ensure that we have the necessary skills to utilize technology effectively.

Leveraging technology is a multifaceted endeavor that requires a strategic approach. By automating tasks, accessing information and resources, fostering collaboration, and staying abreast of the latest trends, we can harness the power of technology to enhance our productivity, creativity, and overall well-being. However, it is essential to strike a balance between embracing technology and maintaining our human connection, ensuring that we do not become overly reliant on digital tools and platforms. By leveraging technology effectively, we can unlock a world of possibilities and create a brighter future for ourselves and generations to come.

Adapting to change is essential for survival and success. Embrace change as an opportunity for growth, remain flexible, and be willing to learn and unlearn. The world is constantly evolving; don't get left behind.

ꝒꝒꝒ

FOURTEEN
CONTINUOUS LEARNING

In the ever-evolving landscape of the 21st century, the importance of continuous learning cannot be overstated. The relentless pace of technological advancements, shifting societal norms, and the emergence of new industries demand that we remain adaptable and constantly update our knowledge and skills. Continuous learning, the ongoing pursuit of knowledge and personal development, is no longer a luxury but a necessity for individuals and organizations alike to thrive in this dynamic world.

At its core, continuous learning is a mindset, a commitment to lifelong growth and development. It is the recognition that our education does not end with a degree or certification but is an ongoing journey that extends throughout our lives. This mindset embraces curiosity, open-mindedness, and a willingness to step outside of our comfort zones to explore new ideas and perspectives.

The benefits of continuous learning are manifold. On a personal level, it enhances our cognitive abilities, improves our problem-solving skills, and boosts our creativity. It keeps our minds sharp, agile, and adaptable, enabling us to navigate the complexities of modern life with greater ease. Furthermore, continuous learning can lead to increased self-confidence, as we acquire new skills and knowledge, expanding our horizons and opening up new possibilities.

In the professional realm, continuous learning is a key driver of career advancement. The job market is constantly evolving, with new technologies and skillsets emerging at an unprecedented pace. Those who embrace continuous learning are better equipped to adapt to these changes, making them more valuable assets to their organizations. By staying up-to-date with the latest trends and developments in their field, professionals can enhance their expertise, improve their performance, and increase their earning potential.

Continuous learning also plays a crucial role in organizational success. Companies that foster a culture of learning are more innovative, adaptable, and resilient. They are able to attract and retain top talent, as employees are drawn to environments that value growth and development. Moreover, continuous learning can lead to increased productivity, improved problem-solving, and enhanced customer service, all of which contribute to the bottom line.

There are numerous ways to engage in continuous learning. Formal education, such as taking courses or pursuing advanced degrees, is one option. However, learning does not have to be confined to the classroom. We can learn through informal channels, such as reading books and articles, listening to podcasts, attending workshops and conferences, or simply engaging in conversations with knowledgeable individuals.

In the digital age, the internet has become a vast repository of knowledge and resources for learning. Online courses, tutorials, and webinars offer a flexible and accessible way to learn new skills and knowledge. Social media platforms can also be valuable tools for connecting with experts, joining online communities, and staying abreast of the latest developments in our field.

Mentoring and coaching are also powerful tools for continuous learning. Learning from experienced individuals can provide valuable insights, guidance, and support. Mentors can share their knowledge and experience, helping us navigate challenges and achieve our goals. Coaching can help us identify our strengths and weaknesses, set realistic goals, and develop strategies for improvement.

Ultimately, continuous learning is a personal journey. It is about identifying our own learning styles and preferences, setting clear goals, and finding the resources and support we need to achieve them. It is about embracing a growth mindset, where we view challenges as opportunities for learning and setbacks as stepping stones to success.

Continuous learning is an essential ingredient for personal and professional success in the 21st century. It empowers us to adapt to change, expand our knowledge and skills, and reach our full potential. By embracing a lifelong commitment to learning, we can navigate the complexities of the modern world with confidence, creativity, and resilience. The journey of learning is a never-ending one, and the rewards are immeasurable.

Your network is your net worth. Build genuine relationships, seek out mentors and collaborators, and leverage the collective wisdom of your community. Together, you can achieve more than you ever could alone.

♡♡♡

FIFTEEN
MAINTAINING MOTIVATION

In the pursuit of any goal, whether it be personal, professional, or creative, maintaining motivation is a crucial factor in determining success. Motivation is the driving force that propels us forward, fueling our efforts and enabling us to overcome obstacles. It is the spark that ignites our passion and the fuel that sustains our perseverance. However, motivation is not a constant state of being; it ebbs and flows, often waning in the face of challenges and setbacks. The ability to maintain motivation, therefore, becomes a critical skill for anyone seeking to achieve their goals.

Motivation can be broadly categorized into two types: intrinsic and extrinsic. Intrinsic motivation stems from the inherent satisfaction and enjoyment we derive from an activity itself. It is driven by our personal interests, values, and passions. For example, a writer who is intrinsically motivated will write because they enjoy the creative process and find fulfillment in expressing their thoughts and ideas. Extrinsic motivation, on the other hand, is driven by external rewards or punishments. It is based on the desire to gain recognition, approval, or material rewards, or to avoid negative consequences. For instance, a student who studies hard to get good grades or an employee who works overtime to earn a bonus is extrinsically motivated.

While both types of motivation can be effective in driving behavior, intrinsic motivation is generally considered to be more sustainable and fulfilling in the long run. When we are intrinsically motivated, we are more likely to persevere in the face of challenges, as we are driven by a genuine interest in the activity itself rather than by external rewards. Extrinsic motivation, while useful in certain situations, can be fleeting and may not sustain us through the inevitable ups and downs of pursuing our goals.

Maintaining motivation requires a multifaceted approach that addresses both intrinsic and extrinsic factors. One of the most effective strategies is to set clear, specific, and meaningful goals. Goals provide a sense of direction and purpose, giving us something to strive for and a benchmark against which to measure our progress. When our goals are aligned with our values and passions, we are more likely to be intrinsically motivated to pursue them.

Breaking down large goals into smaller, more manageable tasks can also help to maintain motivation. This approach makes the goal seem less daunting and provides a sense of accomplishment as we complete each task. Celebrating small victories along the way can boost our confidence and reinforce our commitment to the larger objective.

Creating a supportive environment is another crucial factor in maintaining motivation. Surrounding ourselves with positive and encouraging people who believe in our abilities can provide a much-needed boost when our motivation wanes. Joining a community of like-minded individuals who share our goals can also provide a sense of belonging and camaraderie, fostering a spirit of collaboration and mutual support.

Maintaining motivation also requires a healthy dose of self-care.

Taking care of our physical and mental health is essential for sustained motivation. Getting enough sleep, eating nutritious food, and engaging in regular exercise can all contribute to improved energy levels, focus, and overall well-being. Stress management techniques, such as meditation, yoga, or spending time in nature, can also help to reduce anxiety and promote a positive outlook.

Finally, maintaining motivation requires resilience and a willingness to learn from setbacks. The path to success is rarely a smooth one, and setbacks are inevitable. The key is to view these setbacks as learning opportunities rather than failures. By analyzing our mistakes and adjusting our strategies, we can emerge from setbacks stronger and more determined than before.

Maintaining motivation is an ongoing process that requires a combination of intrinsic and extrinsic factors. By setting clear goals, breaking down tasks into smaller steps, creating a supportive environment, practicing self-care, and learning from setbacks, we can sustain our motivation and achieve our goals. Remember, motivation is not a destination but a journey, and the key is to find what works best for us and to adapt our strategies as needed. With dedication, perseverance, and a positive mindset, we can overcome any obstacle and achieve our dreams.

Healthy habits are the foundation of a vibrant and fulfilling life. Nourish your body with wholesome food, move regularly, prioritize sleep, and manage stress effectively. Take care of yourself, and everything else will fall into place.

♡♡♡

SIXTEEN

THE ROLE OF FEEDBACK

In the intricate tapestry of personal and professional growth, feedback emerges as a thread of paramount importance. It is the mirror that reflects our strengths and weaknesses, the compass that guides us towards improvement, and the catalyst that propels us towards excellence. Feedback, in its various forms, plays a pivotal role in shaping our perceptions, enhancing our performance, and ultimately, enabling us to reach our full potential.

At its core, feedback is information provided to us about our actions, behaviors, or performance. It can be positive, highlighting our strengths and achievements, or constructive, pointing out areas where we can improve. Regardless of its form, feedback serves as a valuable tool for self-awareness and growth. It allows us to gain a deeper understanding of how our actions are perceived by others and how they impact our overall performance.

One of the primary functions of feedback is to identify areas for improvement. Constructive feedback, when delivered thoughtfully and respectfully, can highlight our blind spots, biases, or areas where we may be falling short. It provides us with an opportunity to reflect on our actions, identify patterns of behavior, and make necessary adjustments to improve our performance. By embracing feedback as a learning opportunity, we can continuously evolve and refine our skills, knowledge, and approaches.

Positive feedback, on the other hand, reinforces our strengths and achievements. It acknowledges our efforts, recognizes our contributions, and provides a sense of validation and encouragement. Positive feedback can boost our confidence, motivation, and morale, fueling our drive to continue striving for excellence. It can also help us identify our unique talents and skills, enabling us to leverage them more effectively in our personal and professional lives.

Feedback is not limited to a single source; it can come from a variety of individuals and channels. In the workplace, feedback can be provided by managers, colleagues, subordinates, or even customers. In our personal lives, feedback can come from family members, friends, mentors, or coaches. Each source of feedback offers a unique perspective and can provide valuable insights into our behavior and performance.

The effectiveness of feedback, however, depends largely on how it is delivered and received. Constructive feedback should be specific, actionable, and focused on behavior rather than personality. It should be delivered in a timely manner and in a supportive and respectful tone. Similarly, receiving feedback requires an open mind, a willingness to listen and learn, and a commitment to making positive changes.

The impact of feedback extends beyond individual growth. It also plays a crucial role in building strong relationships, fostering collaboration, and creating a positive and productive work environment. When feedback is exchanged openly and honestly, it can strengthen trust, enhance communication, and resolve conflicts more effectively. It can also promote a culture of continuous improvement, where individuals are encouraged to learn from their mistakes and strive for excellence.

In the digital age, technology has opened up new avenues for feedback. Online platforms, surveys, and social media tools have made it easier than ever to gather feedback from a wide range of sources. However, it is important to remember that not all feedback is created equal. Some feedback may be biased, inaccurate, or simply irrelevant. It is essential to evaluate feedback critically, considering the source, context, and content before deciding how to incorporate it into our personal or professional development.

Feedback is an invaluable tool for growth, development, and success. It provides us with a mirror to see ourselves more clearly, a compass to guide us towards improvement, and a catalyst to propel us towards excellence. By actively seeking and receiving feedback, both positive and constructive, we can gain valuable insights into our strengths and weaknesses, enhance our performance, build stronger relationships, and ultimately, achieve our full potential. Feedback is not merely about criticism or praise; it is about learning, growing, and evolving into the best version of ourselves.

Feedback is a gift. Embrace it with an open mind, learn from it, and use it to fuel your growth. Don't be afraid to ask for feedback, and be willing to give it constructively.

SEVENTEEN

Healthy Habits

Healthy habits are the bedrock of a fulfilling and vibrant life. They encompass a wide range of behaviors and practices that nurture our physical, mental, and emotional well-being. While the specific habits that constitute a healthy lifestyle may vary from person to person, there are certain fundamental principles that apply universally. Incorporating these healthy habits into our daily routines can significantly improve our quality of life, reduce the risk of chronic diseases, and enhance our overall happiness and longevity.

One of the most fundamental healthy habits is maintaining a balanced and nutritious diet. What we eat fuels our bodies and minds, providing the energy and nutrients necessary for optimal functioning. A healthy diet should include a variety of fruits, vegetables, whole grains, lean proteins, and healthy fats. It should also be low in processed foods, sugary drinks, and unhealthy fats. Eating regular meals and snacks throughout the day can help maintain stable blood sugar levels and prevent overeating. Additionally, staying hydrated by drinking plenty of water is essential for numerous bodily functions, including digestion, temperature regulation, and nutrient absorption.

Regular physical activity is another cornerstone of a healthy lifestyle. Exercise not only helps us maintain a healthy weight but also strengthens our muscles, bones, and cardiovascular system. It can also reduce the risk of chronic diseases such as heart disease, stroke, type 2 diabetes, and certain types of cancer. Furthermore, exercise has numerous mental health benefits, including reducing stress, anxiety, and depression, and improving mood and cognitive function. Aim for at least 150 minutes of moderate-intensity aerobic activity or 75 minutes of vigorous-intensity aerobic activity each week, along with muscle-strengthening activities on two or more days a week.

Adequate sleep is crucial for both physical and mental health. During sleep, our bodies repair and restore themselves, while our brains consolidate memories and process information. Lack of sleep can lead to a host of negative consequences, including fatigue, impaired cognitive function, weakened immune system, and increased risk of chronic diseases. Aim for 7-8 hours of sleep per night, and establish a consistent sleep schedule to regulate your body's natural sleep-wake cycle.

Stress management is another vital aspect of a healthy lifestyle. Chronic stress can take a toll on our physical and mental health, contributing to various health problems, including high blood pressure, heart disease, obesity, and depression. Finding healthy ways to manage stress is essential for our well-being. This can include exercise, relaxation techniques such as yoga or meditation, spending time in nature, or engaging in hobbies and activities we enjoy.

Maintaining strong social connections is also crucial for our health and happiness. Humans are social beings, and social isolation can have a detrimental impact on our mental and physical health. Nurturing relationships with family and friends, participating in social activities, and volunteering in our communities can all contribute to a sense of belonging and purpose.

In addition to these core habits, there are numerous other healthy behaviors that can further enhance our well-being. These include maintaining good hygiene, practicing safe sex, avoiding smoking and excessive alcohol consumption, and getting regular checkups and screenings.

Incorporating healthy habits into our lives requires a commitment to change and a willingness to prioritize our well-being. It is not about making drastic changes overnight but rather about making small, sustainable adjustments that we can maintain over time. Setting realistic goals, tracking our progress, and rewarding ourselves for our achievements can help us stay motivated and on track.

Remember, healthy habits are not a destination but a journey. It is about making choices that support our long-term health and happiness, rather than seeking quick fixes or temporary gratification. By embracing a holistic approach to health and well-being, we can create a life that is both fulfilling and sustainable.

Motivation is the engine that drives your actions. Find your passion, set meaningful goals, and create a supportive environment. When your motivation wanes, remember your why and keep pushing forward.

EIGHTEEN

NETWORKING AND COLLABORATION

In today's interconnected world, networking and collaboration have become indispensable for personal and professional growth. The traditional notion of individual achievement is increasingly being replaced by a recognition that collective efforts often lead to greater success and fulfillment. Networking, the process of building relationships and connections with others, and collaboration, the act of working together to achieve a common goal, are two sides of the same coin. They represent a dynamic interplay of human interaction that can unlock a wealth of opportunities, knowledge, and support.

Networking is not merely about collecting business cards or attending social events. It is about building genuine relationships based on mutual respect, trust, and shared interests. It involves connecting with people from diverse backgrounds, industries, and experiences. These connections can provide us with valuable insights, advice, and opportunities that we might not otherwise have access to.

One of the most significant benefits of networking is the expansion of our knowledge and expertise. By engaging in conversations with individuals from different fields, we are exposed to new ideas, perspectives, and approaches. This cross-pollination of knowledge can spark innovation, creativity, and problem-solving skills. Furthermore, networking allows us to tap into the collective wisdom and experience of others, enabling us to learn from their successes and failures.

Networking also opens doors to new opportunities. Whether it's landing a dream job, securing funding for a startup, or finding collaborators for a project, our network can be a valuable source of leads and introductions. The people we know can connect us with the people we need to know, creating a ripple effect of possibilities. In many cases, it is not just what we know but who we know that can make a significant difference in our lives.

Collaboration, on the other hand, is the process of working together with others to achieve a shared goal. It involves pooling our resources, skills, and knowledge to create something greater than the sum of its parts. Collaboration can take many forms, from informal brainstorming sessions to formal partnerships and joint ventures.

The benefits of collaboration are numerous. It allows us to tackle complex problems that would be difficult or impossible to solve alone. By bringing together diverse perspectives and expertise, we can approach challenges from multiple angles and develop more comprehensive solutions. Collaboration also fosters creativity and innovation, as the exchange of ideas and perspectives can spark new insights and approaches.

Furthermore, collaboration can lead to increased efficiency and productivity. By sharing tasks and responsibilities, we can reduce our individual workload and achieve our goals more quickly. Collaboration can also improve the quality of our work, as we can benefit from the constructive feedback and suggestions of our colleagues.

In the modern workplace, collaboration is becoming increasingly important. As organizations become more complex and interconnected, the ability to work effectively with others is a critical skill. Collaboration tools, such as project management software, video conferencing platforms, and online collaboration spaces, have made it easier than ever to collaborate with colleagues, regardless of their location.

Networking and collaboration are essential for personal and professional growth in the 21st century. By building strong relationships and working together with others, we can expand our knowledge, access new opportunities, solve complex problems, and achieve our goals more effectively. The power of collective effort is undeniable, and those who embrace networking and collaboration are well-positioned for success in today's interconnected world.

ÞÞÞ

Breaking down goals is the key to conquering them. Divide and conquer, tackle one step at a time, and celebrate each victory along the way. Remember, the journey of a thousand miles begins with a single step.

♡♡♡

NINETEEN

CELEBRATING PROGRESS

In the relentless pursuit of our goals and aspirations, it's easy to get caught up in the day-to-day grind and lose sight of the progress we've made. We often fixate on the distance that remains between us and our final destination, overlooking the significant strides we've already taken. However, celebrating progress is not merely a feel-good exercise; it's a crucial element of personal and professional growth, fostering motivation, resilience, and a sense of accomplishment.

Celebrating progress involves acknowledging and appreciating the milestones we achieve along our journey. It's about recognizing the effort, dedication, and perseverance that have brought us closer to our goals. Whether it's a small victory or a major breakthrough, each step forward deserves recognition and celebration. By taking the time to pause and reflect on our achievements, we reinforce positive behaviors, boost our self-confidence, and fuel our motivation to continue striving for success.

One of the primary benefits of celebrating progress is the boost it provides to our motivation. When we acknowledge our accomplishments, we reinforce the belief that our efforts are worthwhile and that we are capable of achieving our goals. This positive reinforcement can be incredibly powerful, especially when faced with challenges or setbacks. By reminding ourselves of our past successes, we can reignite our passion and determination to overcome obstacles and continue moving forward.

Celebrating progress also fosters resilience. The path to success is rarely a smooth one, and setbacks are inevitable. However, by acknowledging and celebrating our progress, we build a reservoir of positive experiences that can help us weather the storms of adversity. When we encounter challenges, we can draw upon the memories of our past achievements to remind ourselves that we have the strength and capability to overcome obstacles.

Furthermore, celebrating progress contributes to a sense of accomplishment and fulfillment. When we take the time to appreciate our achievements, we cultivate a sense of gratitude and satisfaction. This can lead to increased happiness, improved well-being, and a greater sense of purpose. By recognizing the value of our efforts, we are more likely to continue pursuing our goals with enthusiasm and dedication.

Celebrating progress can take many forms. It can be as simple as taking a moment to reflect on our accomplishments and acknowledge the effort we've put in. It can involve sharing our successes with friends, family, or colleagues, seeking their support and encouragement. It can also involve rewarding ourselves for our hard work, whether it's indulging in a favorite treat, taking a well-deserved break, or investing in something that brings us joy.

In the workplace, celebrating progress can have a profound impact on team morale and productivity. When organizations recognize and reward the achievements of their employees, it creates a positive and supportive work environment. This can lead to increased engagement, higher job satisfaction, and improved performance. Furthermore, celebrating progress can foster a sense of camaraderie and collaboration, as team members come together to acknowledge and appreciate each other's contributions.

Celebrating progress is a vital component of personal and professional growth. It boosts motivation, fosters resilience, and contributes to a sense of accomplishment and fulfillment. By taking the time to acknowledge and appreciate our achievements, we reinforce positive behaviors, cultivate a positive mindset, and fuel our drive to continue striving for success. Whether it's a small step or a giant leap, every milestone deserves recognition and celebration. So let us not forget to pause, reflect, and celebrate the progress we've made along our journey.

Prioritization is the art of choosing what matters most. Focus your time and energy on activities that align with your values and goals, and let go of what doesn't serve you.

ღღღ

TWENTY

ADAPTING TO CHANGE

In the tapestry of life, change is the only constant. The world around us is in a perpetual state of flux, with technological advancements, societal shifts, and environmental fluctuations constantly reshaping our reality. The ability to adapt to change, therefore, is not merely a desirable trait but an essential skill for navigating the complexities of the modern world. Adapting to change involves not only accepting the inevitability of change but also embracing it as an opportunity for growth, learning, and transformation.

At its core, adapting to change requires a shift in mindset. It involves moving away from a fixed mindset, which views change as a threat or disruption, towards a growth mindset, which sees change as an opportunity for learning and development. A growth mindset allows us to approach change with curiosity, open-mindedness, and a willingness to embrace new ideas and perspectives. It enables us to see challenges as opportunities for growth and setbacks as stepping stones to success.

One of the key aspects of adapting to change is the ability to remain flexible and adaptable. This involves being willing to adjust our plans, strategies, and even our beliefs in response to new information or circumstances. It requires us to let go of rigid expectations and embrace a more fluid and dynamic approach to life. By cultivating flexibility, we become more resilient in the face of change and better equipped to navigate the unpredictable nature of the world.

Another crucial element of adapting to change is the willingness to learn and unlearn. Change often necessitates acquiring new skills, knowledge, and perspectives. It may also require us to unlearn old habits and beliefs that no longer serve us. Embracing a lifelong learning mindset allows us to continuously adapt and evolve, staying relevant and competitive in an ever-changing world.

Adapting to change also involves effective communication and collaboration. Change can often be disruptive, leading to uncertainty, anxiety, and resistance. Open and transparent communication can help alleviate these concerns, ensuring that everyone understands the reasons for the change, the potential benefits, and their role in the process. Collaboration allows us to leverage the collective wisdom and experience of others, fostering a sense of shared purpose and support during times of transition.

Furthermore, adapting to change requires a willingness to step outside our comfort zones. Change often forces us to confront our fears and insecurities, pushing us beyond our familiar boundaries. By embracing the discomfort of the unknown, we open ourselves up to new possibilities and experiences. We discover hidden strengths, develop new skills, and ultimately, grow as individuals.

In the workplace, adapting to change is essential for success. Organizations are constantly evolving to stay competitive in a dynamic market. Employees who can adapt to new technologies, processes, and organizational structures are more valuable to their employers. They are able to embrace change as an opportunity for growth, contributing to the overall success of the organization.

Adapting to change is not always easy. It can be a challenging and sometimes painful process. However, by cultivating a growth mindset, remaining flexible, embracing learning, communicating effectively, collaborating with others, and stepping outside our comfort zones, we can navigate change with greater ease and confidence. The ability to adapt to change is not just a survival skill; it is a thriving skill. It empowers us to embrace the unknown, overcome challenges, and create a more fulfilling and meaningful life.

In the grand scheme of things, change is not something to be feared but to be embraced. It is the force that drives progress, innovation, and evolution. By adapting to change, we not only survive but thrive, creating a brighter future for ourselves and generations to come.

The blueprint for success is unique to you. Embrace your individuality, experiment with different strategies, and create a life that is both fulfilling and meaningful. Remember, the power to shape your destiny lies within you.

♡♡♡

TWENTY-ONE
SUMMARY

In the quest for a life of purpose, productivity, and fulfillment, the power of proactivity emerges as a guiding principle. By taking initiative and actively shaping our destinies, we unlock a world of opportunities for personal and professional growth. This journey begins with setting clear goals, specific and measurable objectives that ignite our passion and provide a roadmap for success.

As we embark on this journey, effective time management becomes our compass. By prioritizing tasks, planning our days, and utilizing techniques like the Pomodoro method and timeboxing, we maximize our productivity and make the most of our finite time. The ability to delegate tasks and resist the allure of multitasking further enhances our efficiency, allowing us to focus on our core responsibilities and priorities.

Along the way, we encounter the formidable foe of procrastination. To overcome this obstacle, we must delve into its root causes, identify our personal triggers, and implement strategies to break down tasks, set deadlines, and reward ourselves for progress. By understanding that procrastination is not simply a matter of laziness but a complex psychological phenomenon, we can develop tailored solutions to overcome it.

The role of mindset in our journey cannot be underestimated. Cultivating a growth mindset, the belief that our abilities can be developed through dedication and hard work, empowers us to embrace challenges, learn from setbacks, and persistently strive for improvement. By fostering a positive outlook and surrounding ourselves with supportive individuals, we create an environment conducive to growth and achievement.

Building a routine is akin to constructing a sturdy framework for our lives. By establishing consistent habits and patterns of behavior, we reduce decision fatigue, overcome procrastination, improve our sleep quality, and create more time for the activities we enjoy. A well-crafted routine provides a sense of structure and predictability, allowing us to focus our energy on what truly matters.

As we progress towards our goals, effective planning becomes our roadmap. By outlining the specific steps, actions, and resources required to achieve our objectives, we create a clear path forward. Anticipating obstacles, continuously monitoring our progress, and leveraging technology further enhance our planning efforts, ensuring that we stay on track and adapt to changing circumstances.

The importance of rest in this journey cannot be overstated. Rest, in its various forms, including sleep, relaxation, and leisure activities, is essential for our physical, mental, and emotional well-being. By prioritizing rest and incorporating it into our daily routines, we recharge our batteries, improve our cognitive function, and enhance our overall performance.

To optimize our focus and productivity, we must also learn to minimize distractions. The modern world is rife with distractions, from the constant pings of notifications to the allure of social media. By setting boundaries, creating a distraction-free workspace, and managing both external and internal distractions, we can cultivate an environment conducive to deep work and meaningful engagement.

Leveraging technology is another key aspect of our journey. By utilizing digital tools and platforms, we can automate tasks, access vast repositories of information, foster collaboration, and stay abreast of the latest trends and developments. However, it is essential to strike a balance between embracing technology and maintaining our human connection, ensuring that we do not become overly reliant on digital tools.

Continuous learning is the lifeblood of personal and professional growth. By actively seeking out new knowledge, skills, and perspectives, we remain adaptable, innovative, and competitive in an ever-changing world. Formal education, informal learning, mentoring, and coaching are all valuable avenues for continuous learning, and the internet offers a wealth of resources for those who are eager to expand their horizons.

As we progress on our journey, celebrating our progress is crucial for maintaining motivation and building resilience. Acknowledging and appreciating our achievements, both big and small, reinforces positive behaviors, boosts our self-confidence, and fuels our drive to continue striving for success. By taking the time to celebrate our wins, we create a positive feedback loop that encourages us to persevere in the face of challenges.

Finally, adapting to change is an inevitable part of life. The world around us is in a constant state of flux, and our ability to adapt to these changes is essential for our survival and success. By cultivating a growth mindset, remaining flexible, embracing learning, and collaborating with others, we can navigate change with grace, resilience, and optimism.

Citation And References

Citation and ReferencesThis book represents the culmination of extensive research and meticulous analysis, incorporating a diverse range of sources, including numerous books, scholarly studies, and personal experiences. Additionally, I have scoured various websites to gather relevant information and data essential for the compilation of this work. I have taken every precaution to ensure the accuracy of the information presented and have diligently cited all sources to acknowledge their contributions.

Despite these efforts, the possibility of inadvertent errors remains. I deeply value the insights of my readers and appreciate any feedback that can help identify and rectify such inaccuracies. I encourage you to bring any discrepancies to my attention.

Your feedback is not only welcome but crucial, as it will aid in correcting current editions and enhancing the content of future ones. I am committed to maintaining the highest standards of accuracy and reliability in my work and thank you for your support and understanding.

Additionally, I firmly uphold the principle of freedom of speech and expression as guaranteed under Article 19(1)(a) of the Constitution of India, and I respect the diverse viewpoints and expressions of all readers.

Other Books Of The Author

1. Empowering Minds: A Journey into Women's Self-Discovery and Power
2. The Dynamics of Motivation: Catalyzing Thought into Action
3. Meditation and Mental Well Being: The Path to Inner Peace and Clarity
4. The Psychology of Child Education: Nurturing Future Generations
5. Ethical Enlightenment: A Modern Guide to Living with Integrity
6. Voices of Empowerment: Stories of Women Rising Against Odds
7. Social Psychology in Everyday Life: Understanding Human Connections
8. The Essence of Motivational Speaking: Inspiring Change in Others
9. Balancing Acts: Women, Work, and the Will to Lead
10. Guiding with Grace: Raising Children with Compassion and Awareness
11. The Power of Positive Aging: Embracing Life After Fifty
12. Building Resilient Communities: Social Work in Action
13. The Ethical Educator: Principles for Teaching and Learning
14. From Insight to Impact: Social Psychology for a Better World
15. The Ethics of Empathy: A Guide to Ethical Living
16. The Science of Empowering the Self: Navigating Life's Challenges with Psychological Wisdom
17. The Mindful Conscious Leader: Meditation Techniques for Modern Management
18. Pioneering Spirit: Women's Pathways to Leadership and Empowerment
19. Feeling to Healing: The Role of Emotional Intelligence in Child Development
20. Transformative Talks and Words of Inspiration: Insights into Motivational Oratory

21. Green Ethics: A Path to Sustainable Living
22. Spiritual Integrity: Navigating Life with Moral Compassion
23. Clean Living, Clean Society: The Ethics of Cleanliness
24. Patriotic Spirits: Building a Nation on Positive Attitudes
25. Innovative Integrity & Vibrant Visions: The Ethical and Entrepreneurial Spirit of Gujarat
26. Youthful Visions, Endless Possibilities: Inspiring Ethics and Motivation in Children
27. Living Your Legacy: How to Motivate Others by Living Your Values
28. Secret of Healing Conversations: Ethical Practices in Counselling and Therapy
29. Creative Kindness: Crafting a Life of Compassion and Creativity
30. The Power of Appreciation: How Gratitude Can Transform Your Relationships
31. Bhagavad-Gita: Messages
32. Science of Art: The New Frontier of Fashion Modernism
33. Vivekananda's Virtues: A Blueprint for Modern Living
34. Empower Her: Navigating the Path to Women's Entrepreneurship
35. The Boundless Classroom: Innovations in Global Education
36. The Language of Leadership: Communicating with Authenticity and Impact
37. The Warrior's Mantra: Deciphering the Hanuman Chalisa
38. Echoes of Empathy: Transformative Stories of Social Service
39. Artful Living: Cultivating Creativity in Your Daily Routine
40. Finding Your Why: Discovering Your Passions and Charting Your Course
41. The Role of Social Media in Shaping Self-Esteem and Interpersonal Relationships among Adolescents
42. Karma's Tapestry: Weaving a Life of Selfless Service
43. Altruistic Alchemy: Transforming Lives Through Giving
44. The Blueprint of Pro-Activeness and Productivity: Crafting Habits for Success
45. The Simplicity with Grounded Wisdom: Embracing Authenticity

in a Complex World

46. Secret of Solopreneur's Odyssey: Navigating the Path to Self-Employment
47. Exploring Tapestry of Peace: Global Perspectives on Harmony
48. The Art and Actions of Connection: Mastering Communication for Impact
49. She Governs and at the Helm: Strategies for Political Empowerment
50. Rising Above and Rising with Grace: A Woman's Roadmap to Career Mastery
51. The Effect of Networking & Connectedness: Building Strategic Alliances for Women
52. Beyond his Barriers: Women Thriving in Male-Dominated Fields
53. Secret of Inner Compass: Navigating Life with Intuition
54. Creative & Pro-Active Muses: A Celebration of Women in the Arts
55. Unburdened: The Art of Releasing the Past
56. Amplified Voices: Speeches of Women that Astonished the World
57. Secret of Manifesting Dreams: A Woman's Guide to Intentional Living
58. Ethics and Value Based Education: Reimagining Japan's School System
59. The Moral Compass Curriculum: A Holistic Approach
60. Tech with Heart: Integrating Ethics into Digital Learning
61. Honoring Virtue: Recognizing Ethical Excellence in Education
62. Raising Good Humans: A Guide to Character Development
63. The Spark Within: Nurturing Creativity in Children
64. The Teenager Whisperer: Navigating Adolescence with Grace
65. Igniting a Passion for Learning: Inspiring Lifelong Curiosity
66. The Habit Lab: Cultivating Positive Behaviors in Children
67. Seeds of Empathy: Fostering Compassion in Young Hearts
68. The Reading Revolution: Inspiring a Love of Books in Children
69. The Learning Brain: Unlocking the Secrets of Student Success
70. Teaching for All: Differentiated Instruction Strategies
71. The Time Alchemist: Mastering Time Management for Peak Performance

72. The Resilience Factor: Transforming Setbacks into Stepping Stones
73. The Healing Touch of Nature: An Introduction to Naturopathy
74. Echoes of the Past: Healing Through Past Life Regression
75. The Spiritual Healer's Handbook: Exploring Energy Medicine
76. Crystal Clarity: Unveiling the Power of Gemstones
77. The Dream Weaver's Guide: Decoding the Language of Dreams
78. Emotional Alchemy: Transforming Pain into Power
79. Sonic Serenity: Harnessing Sound for Stress Relief
80. The Entrepreneur's Playbook: Launching Your Business with Confidence
81. Productivity Unleashed: Time Management Strategies for Entrepreneurs
82. The Problem Solver's Toolkit: Creative Solutions for Business Challenges
83. The Future is Now: Emerging Trends in Business
84. The Curious Explorer: A Child's Guide to Scientific Discovery
85. Digital Pioneers: Empowering Kids in the Tech World
86. The Young Philosopher's Guide: Exploring Life's Big Questions
87. Finding Your Voice: Communication Skills for Confident Kids
88. Nature's Playground: A Child's Guide to Outdoor Adventure
89. Growing a Greener Tomorrow: A Guide to Tree Planting & Conservation
90. Driving with Purpose: Ethical Choices on the Road
91. The Healing Touch: Cultivating Compassion in Healthcare
92. Navigating the Digital Landscape: Ethics in the Age of Social Media
93. The Ethical Closet: A Guide to Sustainable Fashion
94. The Mindful Voyager: Sustainable Travel Practices
95. The Feminine Divine: Honoring the Goddesses of India
96. Sacred Sounds: Chanting Your Way to Inner Peace
97. The Yoga Path: Uniting with the Divine Within
98. Rites of Passage: Creating Meaningful Ceremonies
99. The Chakra System: A Map of Inner Transformation
100. Spiritual Sangha: Finding Community through Satsang and

Bhajan

101. Pilgrimage of the Soul: Spiritual Journeys in India

❧❧❧

Dr. Minakshi Bansal
Social Activist
Ahmedabad, Gujarat, Bharat
minakshiindiag20@yahoo.com

|| LOKAHA SAMASTHAHA SUKHINO BHAVANTU ||

www.ingramcontent.com/pod-product-compliance
Lightning Source LLC
LaVergne TN
LVHW042351150826
845671LV00002B/89

* 9 7 9 8 8 9 4 4 6 1 9 5 3 *